MAIN LINE STEAM
— INTO THE —
1980s

Peter J C Skelton

First published in the United Kingdom in 1984 by
Jane's Publishing Company Limited
238 City Road, London EC1V 2PU

ISBN 0 7106 0310

Printed by Toppan Printing Co (S) Pte Ltd
38 Liu Fang Road, Jurong, Singapore 2262

JANE'S

Front: Stanier's superb 'Coronation' Pacific No 46229 *Duchess of Hamilton* is captured in full flight pounding up 'The Long Drag' in the shadows of the snow-capped Penyghent with the heavy 14-coach '55 Club' 'Cumbrian Mountain Pullman' on 20 February 1982. (*Pete Skelton*) Contax RTS   50mm   Kodachrome 25 f2.8, 1/500

Back: The Great Western Railway's finest traditions are portrayed in this view of Collett's elegant 'Castle' class No 5051 *Drysllwyn Castle*, sweeping around the curve to Wilmcote station with the chocolate and cream vintage 'Sunset' charter train, which ran between Didcot and Stratford upon Avon on 26 January 1980. (*Peter Skelton*) *Contax RTS   50mm   Kodachrome 64   f4, 1/500*

Right: The early morning tranquility surrounding Stokesay Castle is momentarily disturbed by the vision of resplendent GWR 4–6–0 No 5051 *Drysllwyn Castle*, hurrying towards Shrewsbury to haul the first leg of the 'Welsh Marches Pullman' back to Hereford. 9 April 1983. (*Pete Skelton*) *Hasselblad 500CM   80mm   Ektachrome pro 65   f4.5, 1/500*

Introduction

The British steam revival is well established in the mid-1980s and the brilliant efforts of the volunteer preservation groups have been well documented.

In Britain today there is an ever growing following for the popular steam railway. So it was with no real surprise that back in 1971 British Rail relented over its main line steam ban, following sustained pressure by enthusiasts and locomotive owners.

Over the following years organised steam tours on the main lines captured the public's imagination and demand grew even further. This momentum culminated in the formation of the Steam Locomotive Operators Association, who, under the guidance of Bernard Staite, negotiated a programme of steam-hauled tours with British Rail's representative, Mr David Ward. Less busy, scenic routes have been selected, not to interfere with the normal running of scheduled trains, with photo-stops to satisfy the avid photographer.

British Rail too were quick to realise the potential of steam excursions and have successfully marketed their own programme of summer specials, when necessary hiring steam locomotives from the National Collection or from private owners. Today preservation groups have the maximum incentive to renovate their locomotives to British Rail's exacting standards. It is then necessary to get the engine accepted into SLOA's official operating list, which is closely vetted to provide a wide variety of locomotive types which will appeal to the public. Private tours are also possible through BR, provided that financial considerations are made in advance.

The colour pictures displayed over the following pages are a tribute to everyone involved with steam preservation and its promotion, and an appreciation of our railway heritage. It would be appropriate here to mention that with a limited number of engines passed for main line running the most popular of them will feature several times over the various routes covered, but I hope this accurately reflects the enormous following for the locomotives concerned. Emphasis has been given towards sunlit scenes which promote colour at its best, set against the natural scenic landscape so characteristic of each route. I very much hope that in trying to achieve this aim, I have hit upon a pleasant compromise.

Information and booking forms regarding the programme of steam tours, can be obtained by forwarding a 9 × 4″ SAE to:- SLOA Marketing, 104 Birmingham Road, Lichfield, Staffs, WS14 9BW. Information on British Rail's own sponsored tours can be obtained at your nearest main line station.

I would like to extend my grateful thanks to all my friends who share the same appreciation for main line steam, and for forwarding their valued transparencies for inclusion in this book. Also special thanks to Derek Short, Stewart Blencowe, Mike Watts and Ken Harris of Jane's, who has allowed a certain amount of freedom over the project. Finally I would like to dedicate the book to my wife Danuta, whose help and understanding has greatly contributed to the final result.

PETER J C SKELTON
June 1984

This page
The classic duo of Midland Compound 4–4–0 No 1000 and 'Jubilee' 4–6–0 No 5690 *Leander* pound through the snow-clad fells at Ais Gill as they lead a southbound 'Cumbrian Mountain Express' to the summit on 12 February 1983. (*Pete Skelton*)

London–Didcot

The Great Western Railway's most famous locomotive, *King George V*, pioneered the return to steam over British Rail's main lines back in October 1971. Once again No 6000 is entrusted to haul a highly prestigious celebration train. This time the occasion was the 150th anniversary of Paddington station, on 1 March 1978. *King George V* can be seen accelerating the commemorative train away from the capital city, ahead of the 1120 Inter-City HST to Bristol, on its run to Didcot.

Due to incorrect lubrication, *KGV* suffered from a hot box en route and the highly publicised train had to return to Paddington behind a diesel-electric. (*Martin Wilkins*)

Canon EF   50mm   Kodachrome 25 f2.8, 1/500

Opposite

Didcot–Birmingham–Henley in Arden–Stratford upon Avon–Didcot
Two early forms of transport that proved vital in Britain's industrial expansion. Today their respective roles have changed and they now offer an important recreational escape from the frantic pace of the inner cities that they once helped to create.

Traditional long boats, now converted for leisurely cruising, are moored alongside the Oxford Canal with the occupants no doubt alerted by the sound of resplendent GWR 4–6–0 No 5051 *Drysllwyn Castle* passing close by at Lower Heyford with a private charter train from Didcot to Birmingham's Moor Street station. The return run travelled via Henley in Arden and Stratford upon Avon, and took place during one of the finest spring periods since records began. 14 April 1984. (*Pete Skelton*)

*Hasselblad 500CM   150mm
Ektachrome pro 64   f4.5, 1/500*

Above

Birmingham–Didcot–Birmingham
A great deal of experience was gained during the early period of steam-hauled specials over BR main lines. These rare outings paved the way for today's excellent programme of scheduled specials by both SLOA and BR.

A fleeting glimpse of the famous LNER A3 Pacific No 4472 *Flying Scotsman* between the autumn-tinged trees lining the embankment leading to Harbury tunnel is captured by the camera during the Birmingham to Didcot run of the LCGB special on 27 October 1973. (*Martin Wilkins*)

*Pentax SIA   55mm   Kodachrome 11
f2.8, 1/500*

Didcot–Stratford upon Avon–Didcot

On four consecutive Sundays in June 1983, the Great Western Society organised the 'William Shakespeare Express' between Paddington and the famous playwright's home town, Stratford-upon-Avon. 'King' class 4–6–0 *King George V* reflects the early evening light on the approach to Kings Sutton, with the return steam-hauled leg between Stratford and Didcot. 19 June 1983. *(Peter Skelton)*
Hasselblad 2000FC   80mm
Ektachrome pro 64   f2.8, 1/500

Tyseley–Warwick–Tyseley
Built at Swindon to Great Western design by BR in 1950, *Clun Castle* shows the final development of the traditional four-cylinder passenger engine, with its four-row superheater and double chimney. Here No 7029 heads south through the cutting near Lapworth with a shuttle train visiting both the Birmingham Railway museum and Warwick Castle. The special trains, which ran on 3 April 1977, were sponsored by a local newspaper. (*Les Nixon*)
Nikon F   135mm   Kodachrome 25
f4.5, 1/250

Didcot–Stratford upon Avon–Didcot

Left. Sunday maintenance on the approaches to Stratford upon Avon necessitates wrong line working for the Great Western Society's 'Rising Star' charter train from Didcot behind 'Standard' 9F 2–10–0 No 92220 *Evening Star*. In appreciation for extensive repairs undertaken by the society at their Didcot headquarters, the nationally-owned 9F remained as an important attraction at the railway centre for some considerable time, as well as hauling special trains.
13 September 1981. *(Pete Skelton)*
Hasselblad 500CM   80mm
Ektachrome pro 64   f4, 1/500

Opposite. The Great Western Society's 'Sunset' charter train recalls pure GWR nostalgia. In fine traditional style, Didcot's single-chimneyed 'Castle' class 4–6–0 No 5051 *Drysllwyn Castle* pulls away from Stratford upon Avon with the return working to its home depot. This glorious winter day proved to be the last outing to date for the chocolate and cream vintage set, due to the astronomical cost of obtaining an inspection from British Rail to warrant the issue of a main line worthiness certificate.
26 January 1980. *(Pete Skelton)*
Contax RTS   50mm
Kodachrome 25   f2.8, 1/250

Newport–Shrewsbury–Newport
The younger generation, not fortunate enough to remember when steam ruled the rails, now have the opportunity, to absorb the atmosphere of a bygone age when glancing upon Collett's beautifully proportioned 'Castle' class locomotive which is standing in Newport's No 1 platform. The Great Western Society's gleaming 4–6–0 No 5051 *Drysllwyn Castle* awaits the arrival of the Monmouth Railway Society's 25th anniversary commemorative train from Swansea behind a Class 37 diesel, prior to its own run over the North and West route. The organisers of the 'Red Dragon' private charter train to Shrewsbury and back revel in the application of headboards to mark the event. 3 July 1983. (*Pete Skelton*)
Hasselblad 2000FC   80mm
Fujichrome RD100   f4.5, 1/125

Opposite
Chester–Shrewsbury–Hereford–Newport
Retaining a more authentic look is the Severn Valley Railway's new 'Flagship', LMS No 5690 *Leander*, which makes a spirited departure from Shrewsbury. This was the Jubilee's first representative outing for the new owners, and it took charge of an additional SLOA 'Welsh Marches Express' between Chester and Newport on 28 January 1984. (*Pete Skelton*)
Hasselblad 500CM   150mm
Agfachrome R100S   f5.6, 1/500

Bulmers Railway Centre, Hereford

Opposite. Members of the Merchant Navy Loco Preservation Society stand back and admire their charge as SR Rebuilt Pacific No 35028 *Clan Line* emerges from the locomotive shed at Bulmers Railway Centre, Hereford, before transferring to Foregate station to haul an enthusiasts' special northwards.

The highly successful cider company, who had the foresight and courage to have a vested interest in steam, are now extending their factory and building a new two-road engine shed to house an impressive stud of main line engines. (*Pete Skelton*)
Canon FTb, 50mm Kodachrome 64 f4, 1/250

Right. Protected by its own engine shed, *King George V* receives a personal grooming to ensure spotless paintwork and gleaming copper and brasswork at the Bulmers depot at Hereford. The preceding day saw No 6000 head the bottom leg of the 'Welsh Marches Express', between Hereford and Newport, taking over from its stablemate, LMS Pacific No 6201 *Princess Elizabeth*, which had worked the train down from Shrewsbury. 17 April 1982. (*Pete Skelton*)
Hasselblad 500CM 80mm Ektachrome pro 64 f4, 1/30 (hand held)

Opposite. **Newport–Shrewsbury–Newport**
Two representative trains ran between Newport and Shrewsbury on 6 April 1974. The legendary *Flying Scotsman* appropriately hauled 'The Great Northern' train, while 'The Great Western' excursion, as can be seen, was drawn by the immaculate *Pendennis Castle*. No 4079, a classic example of Collett's finest design, speeds through Dorrington using its large diameter drivers to full

advantage on the return journey from Shrewsbury to Newport. (*Hugh Ballantyne*)
Leica M3   50mm   Kodachrome II
f2.5, 1/500

Above.
Shrewsbury–Hereford–Newport–Hereford
On 17 April 1982 GWR No 7812 *Erlestoke Manor*, made her main line debut with Severn

Valley Railway stablemate No 4930 *Hagley Hall*, already an established performer. The two 4–6–0s are seen climbing Llanvihangel bank, with Skirrid Fawr looming in the background, at the head of the 'Welsh Marches Pullman', on the final leg between Newport and Hereford. (*Peter Lockley*)
Contax 139   50mm   Kodachrome 64
f4, 1/500

Shrewsbury–Hereford–Newport–Hereford

Early in 1981 SLOA marketing promoted the 'Welsh Marches Expresses' over the scenic North & West route. The key to the success of these tours lay in the variety of motive power used over the various scenic sections, plus ample opportunities to photograph the train during the runpasts at a designated photo stop. Visiting SR 4–6–0 No 777 *Sir Lamiel*, heading the 'Welsh Marches Pullman', crosses the River Usk for the second time since leaving Newport at The Bryn, a well known location with the local anglers. (*Pete Skelton*)

Hasselblad 500CM   80mm
Agfachrome R100S   f5.6, 1/500

Hereford–Chester–Hereford

On 26 April 1975 two special trains originating from Euston and St Pancras respectively travelled to Hereford via Birmingham, where each train was steam-hauled over the North & West route to Chester by Hereford-based locos 6000 *King George V* and 35028 *Clan Line*.

For the return journey the trains exchanged motive power and the highly efficient *Clan Line* can be seen breezing up Gresford bank with the 'Mayflower'. Bulleid's 'Merchant Navy' class Pacifics remained in service on BR right into 1967, and despite looking grimy and rundown,

gained on their reputation with frequent running into the 90s in a final swan song on the Southern Region. (*Michael Squire*)
Pentax SIa   55mm   Kodachrome II f3.5, 1/250

17

Newport–Chester–Newport

In recognition of the Queen's Jubilee anniversary in 1977, the North & West route witnessed special celebration trains on two consecutive weekends. The northbound trains were designated 'The Western Jubilee' and the returning southbound train 'The Midland Jubilee'. Each special involved locomotives from the four regions: 6000 *King George V*, 35028 *Clan Line*, 6201 *Princess Elizabeth* and 4498 *Sir Nigel Gresley*. LMS maroon Pacific *Princess Elizabeth* momentarily basks in the late afternoon sunlight before plunging into the dark depths of Dinmore tunnel with 'The Midland Jubilee' special on 8 October 1977. (*Stewart Blencowe*) *Mamiya DSX1000   135mm Kodachrome 64   f3.5, 1/500*

Shrewsbury–Hereford–Newport–Hereford
The LMS maroon livery blends well into the season's tarnished hillside behind Church Stretton as 'Jubilee' class 4–6–0 No 5690 *Leander* confidently hauls the southbound WME between Shrewsbury and Hereford.

Leander is making a return visit to the area after undergoing a major overhaul during most of 1981 at the Bridgnorth works of the Severn Valley Railway, whilst still under private ownership. 13 March 1982. (*Pete Skelton*)

Hasselblad 500CM   *80mm*
Agfachrome R100S   *f5.6, 1/500*

Shrewsbury–Hereford–Newport–Hereford

Right. The period between spring and summer sees visiting 2–10–0 class 9F No 92220 *Evening Star* hauling the southbound WME across the Welsh border, near Llangua. It's still the lambing season on the banks of the meandering River Monnow, which leads the passengers to views of the Black Mountains and the stiff climb to Llanvihangel summit just a few miles ahead. 24 May 1982. (*Pete Skelton*)
Hasselblad 500CM
150mm
Ektachrome pro 64
f4, 1/500

Opposite. A familiar location on the Welsh Marches circuit is Stokesay Castle, with its attractive pond situated in front of the fortified manor house. Here we see *King George V*, accelerating away from the Craven Arms photostop with its usual clean exhaust, hauling the WME to Hereford on 18 February 1984. *Leander* was in charge of the train between Newport and Hereford. (*Pete Skelton*)
Hasselblad 2000FC
80mm
Ektachrome pro 64
f4.5, 1/500

Left
Shrewsbury–Hereford–Newport–Hereford
In a determined effort to regain lost time, LMS class 7P Pacific No 6201 *Princess Elizabeth* leaves a vapour trail in its wake between the Long Mynd and Wenlock Edge hills at Marshbrook, with the Shrewsbury to Hereford portion of the WME on 14 February 1981. The final return leg to Newport was entrusted to No 4930 *Hagley Hall*, which also ran in ideal sunny conditions. (*Robert J Green*)
Minolta XD7   100mm
Kodachrome 25
f3.5, 1/250

Opposite.
Hereford–Chester–Hereford
For just two weeks of the year the autumn colours can be seen at their very best, providing you can view on a brilliant sunny day. Such conditions were prevalent on the occasion of LMS 'Black 5' No 5000 passing near the trout farm at Marshbrook with the newly introduced northbound SLOA 'Welsh Marches Pullman' between Hereford and Chester. The return journey was hauled by LMS 'Coronation' class 4–6–2 No 46229 *Duchess of Hamilton*, which was making its inaugural visit to the North & West route on 23 October 1982 (see page 27). (*Pete Skelton*)
Hasselblad 500CM
80mm
Ektachrome pro 64
f4, 1/500

South of Ruabon the magnificent Cefn viaduct spans the River Dee near Newbridge. The vale of Llangollen remains undisturbed by the crossing of the 'Inter City' charter train with SVR mixed traffic pairing of GWR No 4930 *Hagley Hall* and LMS No 5000 at the helm. 22 September 1979. *(Pete Skelton)*
Hasselblad 500CM   80mm
Ektachrome 64   f2.8, 1/250

Shrewsbury–Hereford–Newport–Hereford
Another nicely balanced pair from the impressive Severn Valley stud of locomotives to take to the main line is the popular combination of Standard 2–6–4T No 80079 and the 'Flying Pig', No 43106.

The weather may have been drizzly on 26 February 1983 but spirits were not dampened on the footplates of the engines as they hurry the return working of the 'WMP' away from the brick works at Ponthir with the run up to the Abergavenny photo-stop. (*Pete Skelton*)
Yashica FR1   50mm
Kodachrome 25   f2, 1/250

Opposite.

Hereford–Chester–Hereford

A most advantageous viewpoint to observe the spectacle of passing trains is found on a steep hillside just north of Onibury Crossing. Illustrated here is the SVR's 'Black 5' No 5000, hauling a northbound 'Welsh Marches Pullman' train towards the medieval Stokesay Castle, amid the Autumn colours on 23 October 1982. (*Pete Skelton*)

Hasselblad 500CM	*150mm*
Ektachrome pro 64	*f4.5, 1/500*

Above

York–Chester–Hereford

On 23 October 1982 maroon-liveried LMS 8P Pacific No 46229 *Duchess of Hamilton* had already crossed England with three Pullmans from the National Railway Museum at York before adding SLOA's 'Welsh Marches' set which had previously arrived at Chester behind 4–6–0 No 5000. The 'Duchess' makes her inaugural run over the North & West route with an indefatigable display in lifting the 515 ton train up Gresford bank in record time. (*Peter Lockley*)

Contax 139	*50mm*
Kodachrome 64	*f3.5, 1/500*

Hull–Leeds–Stockport–Chester–Shrewsbury
The beautiful ornate awning supporting the station roof at Northwich frames passing SR 4–6–0 No 777 *Sir Lamiel* with its seven-coach train from Hull to Chester on 5 March 1983. It was here that a locomotive exchange took place with 'Black 5' No 5000 taking over the train for the return journey to Hull. Likewise No 777 transferred to the 'Welsh Marches Pullman' train for the final leg to Shrewsbury. (*Pete Skelton*)
Hasselblad 500CM 80mm
Agfachrome R100S
f2.8, 1/250

Northwich motive power depot

Whenever steam locomotives visit the Manchester or Chester areas, British Rail's Northwich depot usually plays host, stabling them alongside throbbing diesel-electrics. Simmering overnight on the depot is SR 4–6–0 No 850 *Lord Nelson*. In the morning a team of volunteers will clean and prepare the locomotive for its scheduled light engine movement to its home base at Carnforth after a short period working SLOA's 'Welsh Marches' circuit trains.

27 November 1983. (*Brian Dobbs*)
Mamiya 645   80mm
Ektachrome EPY pro 50   f8, 60 seconds

Northwich–Standedge–Leeds–Carnforth

Opposite
After a spell working the North & West route, maroon-liveried *Leander* now heads the 'Trans-Pennine Pullman' towards Knutsford with the run to Leeds via Standedge on 10 April 1982.

A fresh engine took over the train at Leeds for the final leg to Carnforth: *Duchess of Hamilton*, which had the classic 'Caledonian' headboard firmly attached. (*Pete Skelton*)
Hasselblad 500CM
80mm
Ektachrome pro 64
f4, 1/500

Left
Stringent safety precautions are adhered to when working steam-hauled specials beneath the overhead electrified catenary. To enable a path through to Standedge, and then on to Leeds, the 'Trans-Penine Pullman' has to pass under the wires for a short distance. This view shows SR 4–6–0 No 850 *Lord Nelson* selecting its designated path through Altrincham station and no doubt turning a few surprised heads in the town centre. Waiting at Leeds to continue the journey to Carnforth was NELPG's KI 2–6–0 No 2005. 14 November 1981. (*Pete Skelton*)
Hasselblad 500CM
80mm
Agfachrome R100S
f4, 1/250

Above

Liverpool–Eccles–Manchester

Once again the echoes from a 'Coronation' Pacific reverberate along Olive Mount cutting at Edge Hill. The headboard on Stanier's 8P Pacific No 46229 *Duchess of Hamilton* indicates a special VIP train to commemorate the 150th anniversary of the opening of the Liverpool & Manchester Railway on 14 September 1980. The high-ranking dignitaries aboard transferred at Eccles to two period open carriages which were subsequently hauled by the 1838-built 0–4–2 veteran *Lion* to the original Manchester terminus. (*Robert J Green*)

Pentax K1000   135mm
Kodachrome 64   f5.6, 1/250

Opposite

Guide Bridge–Sheffield–York–Leeds–Carnforth

Patches of snow still lie on the high ground of the Pennine Hills as the 'Leander Envoy' passes Buxworth on the climb to Chinley, where a photo stop took place in freezing temperatures. The participants enjoyed superb value, with the 'Jubilee' hauling the train throughout its journey to Carnforth via York. 24 February 1979. (*John S Whiteley*)

Pentax   85mm
Kodachrome 25   f4, 1/250

**Guide Bridge–York–
circular–York–Guide Bridge**
The attractive 1946 LMS
post-war black livery awarded
to passenger engines was
enhanced by the straw and
maroon lining, as shown in this
rear three quarters view of
'Royal Scot' class 4–6–0
No 6115 *Scots Guardsman*,
leaving Chinley with 'The
Yorkshire Venturer'. *Scots
Guardsman*'s last outing proved
to be a complicated affair, for
after arriving at York with the
6000 Locomotive Association
special from Cardiff, the train
then completed a 'York
Circular' tour behind 35028
Clan Line. A second train,
originating from Euston called
'The Yorkshire Ranger' did a
similar York Circular behind
4771 *Green Arrow*, before
returning to Guide Bridge
hauled by Dinting's No 6115
Scots Guardsman. 11 November
1978. (*Hugh Ballantyne*)
Hasselblad 2000FC
80mm   Agfa CT18
f5.6, 1/250

Left
**Sheffield–Manchester–
Blackburn–Hellifield–
Carnforth**
One hundred yards from the
photographer the 'Wyvern
Express', passing near Edale
and headed by ex-Somerset
and Dorset 7F No 13809, was in
full sun but rapidly moving
clouds along the Hope Valley
put paid to the sun's brilliance
just at the wrong moment. (*Pete
Skelton*)
*Hasselblad 500CM   80mm
Agfachrome R100S
f4, 1/500*

Opposite

Guide Bridge–York–Carnforth

On one of those rare days in the Peak District when the Pennine Hills have a clear horizon, LNER 4–6–2 No 4472 *Flying Scotsman* heading 'The Merseyside Express' makes the most of the conditions by tackling the 1 in 100 bank out of Chinley with ease. *Scotsman* hauled the train from Guide Bridge to York, where it took over 'The Comet' excursion from *Sir Nigel Gresley* for the cross-country run to Carnforth on 29 September 1979.

At this period SLOA had to rearrange its programme of steam rail tours due to the Penmanshiel Tunnel disaster. (*Pete Skelton*)

Hasselblad 500CM   80mm
Ektachrome 64   f4, 1/500

Above

Sheffield–Leeds–Sellafield–Carnforth

Much of 1981 saw *Leander* out of action while a major overhaul took place at Bridgnorth on the Severn Valley Railway. It was therefore good to see No 5690 make a welcome return to the main line scene on 5 December 1981. *Leander* treads the former Midland Railway main line through Cudworth, which still retains its semaphore signals, en route from Sheffield to Sellafield via Leeds with the Leander Pullman No 2 special.

This stretch of line is no longer used for regular passenger traffic and only on very rare occasions are steam specials allowed over the route. (*Les Nixon*)

Nikon F   135mm   Kodachrome 25
f4, 1/250

York–Leeds–Rochdale–Leeds–York

There has been a gap of 14 years since steam forged a path over the former L & YR Calder Valley main line. Since *Flying Scotsman*'s earlier run, the distinction now goes to MR Compound 4–4–0 No 1000 which can be seen bursting into the sunshine as she crosses Gauxholme viaduct, climbing towards Todmordon with British Rail's seven-coach private charter train on 28 September 1983. The journey from York started with dull conditions, and on reaching the Calder Valley south of Leeds, the crimson lake Compound was shrouded by hill mists. Fortunately before reaching its destination at Rochdale, the sun broke through. (*Keith Francis*)
Pentax K1000   135mm
Kodachrome 64, f3.5, 1/500

Northwich–Standedge–Leeds–York

The *Duchess of Hamilton*, takes things easy even on the stiff climb to Standedge tunnel with 'The Hadrian Pullman' special between Northwich and York. This caution followed a visit to the former LMS workshops at Crewe, where No 46229 received attention to a driving wheel and an overheating bearing.

This particular tour appealed to railway enthusiasts in general, for at York a Deltic took over the train for a run over the East Coast Main Line. 18 July 1981. (*Pete Skelton*)

Hasselblad 500CM   80mm
Ektachrome 64   f2.8, 1/500

Above

Hull–Scarborough–York

Hull Paragon station, with its five elliptical arches, is the starting point for the newly marketed 'Yorkshire Pullman' train, which embraces the Scarborough–York circuit. Proudly heading the first train is HLPG's superbly restored 'King Arthur' class 4–6–0 No 777 *Sir Lamiel*, making a sure-footed departure on 18 September 1982. (*Pete Skelton*)

Contax RTS   50mm
Kodachrome 25   f3.5, 1/250

Opposite

Leeds–Harrogate–York–Scarborough–York–Leeds

Hull Dairycoates-based 'Black 5' No 5305 dashes through the countryside in the spring sunshine at Kirkham Abbey with a new lease of life after being painstakingly restored by the Hull Locomotive Preservation Group. This was its inaugural run with a special train from Leeds to the coastal resort of Scarborough, before finally returning to Leeds. 30 April 1977. (*Martin Wilkins*)

Canon EF   50mm
Kodachrome 25   f3.5, 1/250

46

York–Carnforth–York
The transfer of LMS 4–6–0 No 5...
to Carnforth after a stint at w...
...borough trains resulted in a conv...
...sion which was appropriately name...

Right
York–Harrogate–Leeds–York–Scarborough–York
The peace and tranquility of the early morning is disturbed as Stanier 8P Pacific No 46229 *Duchess of Hamilton* thunders westwards across the splendid viaduct spanning the River Nidd at Knaresborough. The train is the popular BR-sponsored summertime 'Scarborough Spa Express', running from York to Leeds via Harrogate, then back to York before finally continuing to Scarborough. The return trip added up to a total mileage of 212, all behind steam! 19 August 1982. (*Chris Milner*)
Canon AE-1   50mm
Kodachrome 64   f4.5, 1/250

Opposite
York–Leeds–Harrogate–York
A marvellous event that took place during 1979 was the appearance of the National Railway Museum's train of historic catering vehicles. This special composite train was organised by British Rail's Travellers' Fare to celebrate 100 years of on-train catering.
    LNER apple green V2 No 4771 *Green Arrow* passes Kirk Hammerton with the 'Centenary Express' during a run over the York circular route on 29 September 1979. This same day saw sister LNER engines *Flying Scotsman* and *Sir Nigel Gresley* converge on York Station with 'The Merseyside Express' and 'The Comet' excursions. (*Pete Skelton*)
Hasselblad 500CM   80mm
Ektachrome pro 64   f4,   1/ 500

48

York–Harrogate–Leeds

The running of the Ford company's private executive charter train over the York circular route recreated a scene from an earlier railway period. The train consisted of LMS corridor brake No 5155, and BR Pullman vehicles *Eagle* and *Emerald*, while at the rear a Mk1 restaurant car was used for the preparation of meals. The immaculately turned out MR Compound 4–4–0 No 1000 elegantly pulls away from Harrogate with its distinguished train before disembarking the wined and dined businessmen and their wives at Leeds. 7 October 1981 (*Pete Skelton*)

Hasselblad 500CM   80mm
Ektachrome pro 64   f4, 1/500

York–Gascoigne Wood–York

The footplate crew on the famous 'race to the North' star, ex-LNWR 2–4–0 No 790 *Hardwicke*, drop the fire at York after a successful test train down to the freight yard at Gascoigne Wood with MR Compound 1000 and an aged six-wheeled coach from the National Railway Museum on 14 April 1976. These preparations were in readiness for a nine-coach special train which the two period locomotives hauled from York to Carnforth on 24 April. This movement enabled the engines to have a new convenient base for specials which were being run in the area. The most reliable engine proved to be the diminutive 'Precedent' class No 790 *Hardwicke*, which hauled trains over the Furness line, as well as celebrating the centenary of the Settle and Carlisle line with *Flying Scotsman* on 1 May 1976. (*Les Nixon*)

*Leica M3   50mm   Kodachrome 25
f5.6, 1/30*

Left

**Middlesbrough–Newcastle–
Carlisle–Skipton**
A marathon journey lay ahead of
NELPG's 2–6–0 class K1 No 2005
and its Pullman train, with a run from
Middlesbrough to Skipton via
Carlisle on 22 January 1983.
    The apple green-liveried K1 makes
a determined effort to get on with the
job with an energetic departure from
Sunderland, the spectacle highlighted
by the early morning appearance of the
winter sun. (*Peter A Thorne*)
Fujica ST601   55mm
Kodachrome 64   f4, 1/250

Opposise

**Middlesbrough–Newcastle–
Carlisle–Hellifield**
The early morning sun reflects off
Class K1 2–6–0 No 2005 as its
NELPG members work frantically to
prepare their charge during a respite at
Newcastle Central station on
22 January 1983.
    Patrons on the epic excursion now
have time to admire their haulage
locomotive at close quarters before
setting off on the next stage of the
journey along the little used steam
approved route to Carlisle. (*Pete
Skelton*)
Hasselblad 500CM   80mm
Agfachrome R100S   f5.6, 1/250

Opposite
York–Harrogate–Leeds–York
The cold March air accentuates the exhaust from *Green Arrow* in a spectacular fashion as the LNER V2 storms out of Marsh Lane cutting, Leeds, with an enthusiasts special over the York circular route on 15 March 1978. This excursion proved to be an excellent running-in turn prior to the V2's important first assault of the Settle and Carlisle line, which had not been conquered by steam since BR's '15 Guinea Special' train, back in August 1968. (*John S Whiteley*)
*Pentax   85mm   Kodachrome 25
f3.5, 1/250*

Above
Carlisle–Hellifield–Carnforth
A most advantageous spot for a panned view of a locomotive in action is found midway to the summit of Giggleswick bank. Here for example is a fine study of No 5407 tackling the steep gradient with the bottom section of a south-bound 'Cumbrian Mountain Express', between Hellifield and Carnforth on 28 March 1981. (*Hugh Ballantyne*)
*Leica M4–2   50mm   Kodachrome 25
f2, 1/60*

Leeds–Hull–Scarborough–York

Bystanders near the lineside cannot fail to be impressed by the sight of an immaculately turned out locomotive working hard in the crisp morning air, with its pure white exhaust cascading behind. The train is the 'Santa Steam Pullman', seen accelerating through Cross Gates on the Leeds to Hull section. HLPG's other restored loco, No 5305 continued the Pullman train on to Scarborough and York, a fitting end to the year on 29 December 1982. (*Peter A Thorne*)

Fujica ST601   135mm   Kodachrome 64 f3.5, 1/250

56

Hull–Leeds–Carnforth–Sellafield–Hull
This is another occasion when a 'Santa Steam' special ran in spectacular light. 'Black 5' No 5305, ran solo from Hull to Leeds, from where it double-headed the Stephenson Link version No 4767 to Carnforth. The superb combination can be seen hard at work lifting the special up the climb at Bell Busk, with the exhaust masking out the landscape. The leading engine, No 5305, came off at Carnforth to be serviced and turned, while 4767 continued alone to Sellafield. A third 'Black 5', No 5407, returned the train to Carnforth, where once again HLPG's own 5MT No 5305 made the solo run back home. 27 December 1980. (*John S Whiteley*)
Pentax   135mm   Kodachrome 64 f4.5, 1/250

57

Above

Carnforth–Hellifield–Carlisle

The ever-popular LMS 4–6–0 Class 5 No 5407 crosses Arkholme viaduct, where the waters of the River Lune begin to subside now that summer approaches. The 'Black 5' has been entrusted once again with the bottom leg of the northbound 'Cumbrian Mountain Pullman', between Carnforth and Hellifield, on 1 May 1982. (*Keith Francis*)

Pentax K1000   50mm   Kodachrome 64
f4, 1/500

Opposite

Sheffield–Manchester–Blackburn–Hellifield–Carnforth

On a beautiful evening in October, ex-S&DJR 2–8–0 class 7F No 13809 briskly sets away from Hellifield with 'The Wyvern Express', which had originated from Sheffield earlier in the day. The freight engine was negotiating the last section of its long journey to Carnforth, where it would be stabled to work excursions on future dates. 31 October 1981. (*Pete Skelton*)

Hasselblad 500CM   80mm
Ektachrome pro 64   f2.8, 1/500

Carnforth–Hellifield–Carlisle–Hellifield–Carnforth
LNER Class A3 Pacific No 4472 *Flying Scots-man* gets fully into her stride near Mewith, knowing that the climb ahead to Clapham will get even more tough. *Scotsman* was called upon to haul the Carnforth to Hellifield section of the 'Leander Enterprise' special. *Leander* itself completed a 'up and back' trip over the Settle and Carlisle line on 26 April 1980. *(Pete Skelton)*
Contax RTS 50mm Kodachrome 64 f4, 1/500

Northwich–Standedge–Leeds–Carnforth
The spring sunshine escorted *Leander* with the 'Trans Pennine Pullman' from Northwich to Leeds, but the farther north the train progressed, so did the rain clouds increase. It was therefore quite a surprise to catch a sudden burst of sunlight just as *Duchess of Hamilton* approached, sporting the classic 'Caledonian' headboard, during the climb up Giggleswick bank. (*Pete*

Skelton)
Hasselblad 500CM   80mm
Agfachrome R100S   f4, 1/500

Right

Carnforth, Steam Town depot
Unrebuilt 'West Country' class No 34092 *City of Wells* blows off impatiently in front of Carnforth's coaling tower. The Brunswick green Pacific is decorated in Stewarts Lane's prestigious 'Golden Arrow' attire, and stands in −15°C freezing temperatures to await the arrival of the delayed SLOA Pullmans which formed the K&WVR special on an unforgettable 12 December 1981 (see page 58). (*Dave Dyson*)
Mamiya C220   80mm
Ektachrome pro 64   f8, 1/125

Opposite

Carnforth–Ravenglass–Carnforth
Thompson's LNER version of a class '5' mixed-traffic locomotive takes the form of B1 4–6–0 No 1306 *Mayflower*. The B1 pilots the perfectly matching apple green-liveried V2 class 2–6–2 No 4771 *Green Arrow* out of Grange over Sands, reflecting the rapidly descending sun on 21 June 1975.

The enthusiasts aboard are being treated to views across Morecambe Bay during the journey home after visiting the Ravenglass and Eskdale narrow gauge railway. (*Pete Skelton*)
Canon FTb   50mm
Kodachrome X   f4, 1/500

Overleaf

Left. The soft exhaust beats emitted from the multiple jet blastpipe via the large diameter chimney of Southern Railway 4–6–0 No 850 *Lord Nelson* disguises the actual power produced from the four cylinders. The malachite green-liveried express engine draws 'The Lancastrian' special around the curve shortly after leaving Millom on the outward journey from Carnforth to Sellafield. This particular train was run for the disappointed railfans who had previously been booked on a steam special which ran throughout with a diesel pilot due to a fire risk ban on 17 May 1980. The return journey which was hauled on this glorious summer day by LMS '7P' No 6201 *Princess Elizabeth* can be seen on page 67. 25 August 1980. (*John S Whiteley*)

Pentax   85mm   Kodachrome 25   f4, 1/250

Right. After the Rocket 150 celebrations at Rainhill at the end of May 1980, LMS 'Princess Royal' class Pacific No 6201 *Princess Elizabeth* stayed in the North West during the summer months to work trains from Carnforth's Steamtown depot, culminating in a trip over the S & C line before moving back south to Hereford on 27 September 1980. Before going home *Princess Elizabeth* can be seen returning 'The Lancastrian' special train to Carnforth across the Eskmeals viaduct on 25 August 1980. (*John S Whiteley*)

Pentax   55mm   Kodachrome 25   f4, 1/250

Carnforth–Sellafield–Carnforth

Left. It has become a tradition now during the period immediately after Christmas for SLOA to provide a 'Santa Steam Special' with Santa himself aboard to provide the children with additional gifts. On several of the yearly excursions the weather has been exceptionally clear and one hopes that this tradition continues also.

Superb LNER streamlined greyhound Pacific No 4498 *Sir Nigel Gresley* races up the testing Lindal Bank with the Carnforth to Sellafield run, with the crew revelling in the challenge, on 30 December 1978. Due to the lack of turning facilities at Sellafield, Gresley's 'other' Pacific, *Flying Scotsman*, took charge of the return journey. (*Pete Skelton*)

Hasselblad 500CM   80mm
Agfachrome pro 50S   f4.5, 1/500

Opposite. On 28 December 1982 it was the turn of LNER apple green A3 Pacific No 4472 *Flying Scotsman* to haul the 'Santa Steam Pullman' from Carnforth to Sellafield, again during a fine spell of weather. Having just ambled across the Leven Estuary, *Scotsman* accelerates the train between the fine semaphore signals at Plumpton Junction, where the Windermere–Lakeside branch left the Furness main line prior to its closure in 1967. Part of this line has been retained as the Lakeside and Haverthwaite Railway. SR 4–6–0 No 850 *Lord Nelson* waited at Sellafield to haul the return Pullman train. (*Peter Lockley*)

Contax 139   50mm
Kodachrome 64   f2.8, 1/500

Carnforth–Hellifield–Carlisle

The magnificent Batty Moss viaduct at Ribblehead epitomises the Settle and Carlisle line. The viaduct stands as a living monument to the Victorian engineers and to the men who lost their lives building the massive structure. It is sad to reflect that in 1984 this superb structure was posed to contribute to the line's downfall, due to BR's argument that the high repair costs needed to maintain this and other civil engineering features were not justified by traffic levels. However on 28 November 1981 the viaduct had never looked better than in this view of LNER Class A4 streamlined Pacific No 4498 *Sir Nigel Gresley*, chasing ahead of the darting shadows with the northbound CMP. (*John Cooper-Smith*)
Mamiya 645   150mm
Ektachrome pro 64   f4.5, 1/250

Hellifield–Carlisle–Newcastle–Middlesbrough
A tough start for apple green-liveried 2–6–0 Class K1 No 2005 with its return journey to Middlesbrough, having to tackle the S & C line first. The small class 5 locomotive shows a lot of heart as it hauls the nine-coach Pullman train alongside the attractive River Ribble at Helwith Bridge on 20 March 1983. During a two-month stay at Carnforth, the K1 made outings on the main line to Hellifield, as well as a visit to the Keighley & Worth Valley Railway. (*Pete Skelton*)
Yashica FR1   50mm
Kodachrome 25   f2.8, 1/250

Carlisle–Hellifield–Carnforth

The first section of line for southbound 'Cumbrian Mountain' trains travelling between Carlisle and Appleby passes through the lovely Eden Valley, with its fertile farmlands situated between the Lake District to the west and the Pennines on the east.

At Appleby the SLOA train takes on water after several photographic run-pasts, then gets down to the serious business of the climb up to Ais Gill summit. Here we can see LMS 4–6–0 No 5690 *Leander*, showing a lot or urgency at the head of the CMP as the 'Jubilee' passes under an occupation bridge before plunging into Helm tunnel, as it digs in for the task that lies ahead. 23 January 1982. (*Pete Skelton*)
*Contax RTS   50mm   Kodachrome 25
f2.5, 1/500*

Sheffield–Leeds–Hellifield–Carlisle

In the days of BR steam over the S & C route, the crack train of the day was 'The Thames–Clyde Express'. The former premier train now has premier motive power to re-create the spirit of the past.

No 46229 *Duchess of Hamilton* shows that she is complete master of her train by forging a fast ascent through Horton-in-Ribblesdale with 520 tons in tow. Observers on the train recorded that the powerful Pacific did not reduce its speed at any time during its assault on the climb, and had a marvellous non-stop run to Appleby.

The train had originated from Sheffield behind Class 5 No 5305, which took the 'Thames–Eden Pullman' to Leeds. It was here that the locomotive and headboard were changed for the run to Carlisle on 26 March 1983. (*Pete Skelton*)
Yashica FR1   50mm   Kodachrome 25 f2.8, 1/500

73

Carlisle–Hellifield–Carnforth

The legendary Settle and Carlisle line, with its long, continuous gradient at 1 in 100, tests a locomotive's performance to the very limit. So it was with a little trepidation that British Rail first allowed Bulleid light Pacific No 34092 *City of Wells*, with its revolutionary chain-driven valve gear, over 'The Long Drag', especially in the knowledge that the class was notorious for slipping. Their fears were unfounded, for *City of Wells* passed the test with flying colours and on a wet rail too. The 'West Country' has proved to be a star attraction wherever she goes, and has earned a reputation for putting on spectacular visual displays, as can be seen in this picture of 34092 pounding southwards away from Waitby with the 'Cumbrian Mountain Express' on 10 December 1983.

Another Southern engine, No 850 *Lord Nelson*, completed the Hellifield–Carnforth section in darkness. *(Pete Skelton)*
Yashica FR1   135mm   Kodachrome 25 f2.8, 1/250

Carlisle–Hellifield

The grandeur of the S & C route is evident in this view of the Brunswick green streamlined Pacific No 60009 *Union of South Africa* heading south towards Mallerstang, after leaving Birkett tunnel.

The much-awaited appearance of 'No 9' south of the Border after some 20 years proved to be such a draw for SLOA that it was necessary to arrange hastily additional tours to help satisfy the demand. (*Pete Skelton*)

Hasselblad 2000FC   80mm
Fujichrome pro 50   f4, 1/500

Left
Carlisle–Hellifield–Carnforth
Spectacular light conditions prevailed at Whernside, with the setting sun catching the front of *City of Wells* full in the face, as the Bulleid light Pacific makes a dramatic departure away from the Garsdale water stop with the southbound CME on 10 December 1983. (*Colin Binch*)
Pentax MX   200mm
Fujichrome RD100
f4, 1/250

Opposite

Top
Carlisle–Hellifield–Leeds
Having used her 8P classification to good effect earlier in the day on the climb to Ais Gill summit, *Duchess of Hamilton* can now take things easy on the embankment at Ribblehead, with the southbound CME on 7 January 1984. The rapidly setting sun warms the troubled sky over Whernside, masking the reality of a bitterly cold winter day. (*Pete Skelton*)
Hasselblad 500CM
150mm
Agfachrome R100S
f5.6, 1/500

Bottom
Carnforth–Hellifield–Carlisle
Strong crosswinds continually bring the worst of the weather to lash against the Batty Moss viaduct at Ribblehead. It is therefore not surprising to see LNER No 4498 *Sir Nigel Gresley* battle against the grades and a forceful wind when accelerating the CMP towards the desolate Blea Moor, after recovering from the viaduct's speed restriction on 28 November 1981. The Carnforth–Hellifield leg saw 'WC' No 34092 *City of Wells* complete its inaugural main line run. (*Pete Skelton*)
Contax RTS   135mm
Kodachrome 64
f2.8, 1/500

Carlisle–Hellifield–Carnforth

One of the main highlights of 1982, was the appearance of HLPG's restored SR 4–6–0 No 777 *Sir Lamiel*. However, as a precautionary measure for its first revenue-earning run over the telling S & C route on 3 April 1982, the untried 'King Arthur' joined forces with the trusty LMS Class 5 No 5407. The 4–6–0 pair consolidate their efforts with the southbound working of the CMP as they burst from under the road bridge at Cotehill. *Sir Lamiel* was in fact allowed to do most of the hard work on the arduous climb to prove its capabilities. (*Pete Skelton*)

Contax RTS   135mm   Kodachrome 64 f3.5, 1/250

Carnforth–Hellifield–Carlisle

When it comes to preservation, it pays dividends to do the job properly first time round. Take the case of 'West Country' class Pacific No 34092 *City of Wells*: a dedicated, patient working party over many years have brought their charge up to exacting main line standards. The reward for their labour can be seen in this view of *City of Wells* lifting the northbound CMP train near Foredale, with a strong following wind compacting the impressive exhaust.

The locomotive has built up a fine reputation for its exploits over the main line, and has brought prestige to its owners and supporters and to the K&WVR, plus of course a little revenue which will help with future maintenance costs. (*Pete Skelton*)

Contax RTS   *135mm*   *Kodachrome 64*
f4, 1/500

81

Carlisle–Hellifield–Carnforth

1982 proved a busy year for LMS No 5690 *Leander*, for the locomotive managed to haul SLOA excursions over four of the major steam routes. After passing over Armathwaite viaduct the 'Jubilee' sweeps into the curve before diving into the depths of Baron Wood tunnel, no doubt frightening a few sheep in the process. (*Robert J Green*)

Minolta XD7   *100mm*   *Kodachrome 25*
f3.5, 1/250

Hellifield–Carlisle–Newcastle–Middlesbrough
The apple green Class K1 No 2005 takes a well-earned breather after mastering the Ais Gill challenge, breezing through Kirkby Stephen station on a beautiful afternoon which allowed clear views of Mallerstang Edge and the high fells at their very best. By the time NELPG's engine had reached Carlisle with SLOA's umber and cream Pullman train the light had rapidly diminished, so the rest of the journey to Middlesbrough was in darkness. 20 March 1983. *(Pete Skelton)*
Yashica FR1   50mm   Kodachrome 25
f2.8, 1/500

Opposite

Carlisle–Hellifield–Carnforth

Making a welcome return to the Settle and Carlisle line after an absence of six years is the powerful Standard 2–10–0 No 92220 *Evening Star*.

This event coincided with a difficult period for the organisers of steam tours due to fire risks following a long drought. The miners' strike also inhibited the use of suitable steaming coal. This could account for the smoke effect caused by the hard working fireman as his efforts lift the southbound 'CME' through Baron Wood on Easter Monday 23 April 1984. (*Pete Skelton*)

Hasselblad 500CM   150mm
Fujichrome pro 100   f5.6, 1/500

Above

Carnforth–Hellifield–Carlisle

The timing of the northbound 'Cumbrian Mountain' trains coincides with the best of the afternoon light in which to view the magnificent Yorkshire Dales. With the assault of Ais Gill behind her, the 'Duchess' now passes through Culgaith in the Eden Valley on the gentler run to Carlisle, just as the sunset breaks across the horizon, a colourful end to the day on 29 October 1983. (*Pete Skelton*)

Yashica FR1   50mm   Kodachrome 25
f2.8, 1/500

Edinburgh–Leuchars–Dundee–Stirling–Edinburgh
Above. The photographer was invited by John Cameron, owner of A4 Pacific No 60009 *Union of South Africa*, to travel on the footplate between Edinburgh and Dundee. The journey entailed crossing over both the Forth and Tay Bridges with the SVR thirteen-coach railtour on 29 November 1980.

This privileged view shows the two most famous railway sights in Scotland, with the A4 making good headway across the massively constructed Forth Bridge. (*Jeff M Cogan*)
Canon FTb, 28mm   Ektachrome 400   f3.5, 1/250

Left. **Carlisle Upperby depot**
LMS 4–6–0 No 5305 rests overnight at Carlisle's Upperby depot on 28 December 1983 after bringing to the border city the 'Santa Steam' special on a solo run from Hellifield. The next day saw the Class 5 returned south to Hellifield with the eleven-coach special. It was here that a complete change of motive power took place when green-liveried Class 40 diesel No D200 (40122) powered the train on to Carnforth. (*Pete Skelton*)
Hassleblad 2000FC   80mm   Agfachrome R100S
f5.6, 60 seconds, and four open flashes

Opposite. **Inverness–Kyle of Lochalsh**
The natural beauty and scenery of Scotland often defies words. The picture speaks for itself with this view of the Strathspey Railway's 'Black 5' No. 5025 skirting Loch Carron near Plockton with 'The Ravens Rock Express' from Inverness to Kyle of Lochalsh on 25 September 1982. (*Colin Binch*)
Pentax KX   50mm   Kodachrome 25   f2.8, 1/500

Right
**Inverness–
Kyle of Lochalsh**
Nature plays its part in entertaining the passengers with its subtle hues among the autumn colours of the forest near Raven Rock. The train was privately chartered by the Toyota Motor Company, who commissioned the LMS Class 5 No 5025 on four consecutive days to run over the dramatic Kyle line in the West Highlands. 5 October 1982. (*John Cooper-Smith*)
Mamiya 645   150mm
Ektachrome pro 64
f4, 1/125

Opposite
Falkirk–Dundee–Falkirk
The compact proportions of the Gresley D49 class 4–4–0 are shown to good effect with this silhouette of No 246 *Morayshire* approaching Larbert after its return trip from Falkirk to Dundee on 27 December 1980. *Morayshire* was loaned to the Scottish Railway Preservation Society by its private owner to be returned to steam and is retained north of the Border, where the locomotive has worked throughout its career. (*John S Whiteley*)
Pentax   85mm
Kodachrome 25   f4, 1/250

Fort William–Mallaig–Fort William
After an absence of 21 years, steam once again appears along probably the most scenic line in Britain. Running from the foot of Ben Nevis at Fort William, the Mallaig Extension passes through a dramatic West Highland landscape of mountain and loch to reach the small fishing port and ferry terminal of that name on the Sound of Sleat.

Pictured here on 27 May 1984 is Carnforth's 'Black 5' No 5407 skirting the end of Loch Eilt with the 'West Highlander' during the first day of revenue-earning service. (*Pete Skelton*)
Hasselblad 2000FC   80mm
Fujichrome pro 50   f4, 1/500

Mossend–Stirling–Perth–Edinburgh

The start of a particularly bad spell of severe wintry conditions to hit Scotland coincided with LNER A4 Pacific No 60009 *Union of South Africa*'s outing on the main line with 'The Fair Maid' special on 14 January 1984. The fall of snow managed to bleach out the landscape and contrasted with No 9's nicely burnished Bruns- wick green livery as John Cameron's pride approaches Cumbernauld with the somewhat delayed special from England. (*Pete Skelton*)

Hasselblad 2000FC   80mm
Fujichrome RD100   f4, 1/375

Left.

Fort William–Arisaig–Fort William

Spectacular scenes took place in the West Highlands during the inaugural running of steam-hauled trains between Fort William and Mallaig. Unsuperheated NB 0–6–0 No 673 *Maude* fights for adhesion up the tortuous incline leading to Glenfinnan station with the towering mountains dwarfing the diminutive J36 and its four-coach 'West Highland' train. The severe gradients along the picturesque line made 'Maude' work extremely hard, resulting in a few trackside fires which burnt away the dead winter undergrowth. It also proved necessary to replenish the tender with the cool waters from one of the lochs on the return journey. 28 May 1984. (*Pete Skelton*)
Hasselblad 2000FC
80mm
Fujichrome pro 50
f4, 1/500

Opposite

Kilmarnock– Carlisle–Hellifield– Blackburn–Bold Colliery

A glorious hot, sunny day witnessed the marathon journey on 17 May 1980 of NBR 0–6–0 No 673 *Maude*, travelling from Kilmarnock to Bold Colliery, Lancashire with two Caledonian coaches in readiness for the 'Rocket 150' celebrations. The J36 is seen here passing through the scenic Drumlanrigg Gorge. (*John S Whiteley*)
Pentax   85mm
Kodachrome 25
f4.2, 1/250